Table Of Contents

Foreword

Chapter 1:
Email Marketing Basics For Net work Marketing

Chapter 2:
Getting Subscribers

Chapter 3:
Reducing Unsubscribes

Chapter 4:
Using Transactional Emails

Chapter 5:
Using Triggers In The Email

Chapter 6:
Testing Different Variations Of Your Email

Chapter 7:
Use Analytics To Separate Buyers From NonBuyers

Chapter 8:
Use Loyalty Programs

Chapter 9:
Determine The Correct Frequency To Send Emails

Wrapping Up

Foreword

Staying competitive is very important in any business environment and this is more so relevant when applied to the world of internet marketing. Using the email marketing tool is a good start in the right direction. This style of direct marketing a message is both quick and effective when comparisons are made with other available platforms. Get the info here.

Max Impact Email Marketing
Network Marketing Lead Generation Secrets

Chapter 1:

Email Marketing Basics For Net work Marketing

Synopsis

Reaching the target audience with email marketing strategies will provide several positive and beneficial liaisons. Some of these include enhancing the relationships of the merchant and customer pools, encouraging the customer loyalty and thereby effectively ensuring repeat business.

There is also the avenue to pursuing new customers this way as it creates the circumstances to reach the said customer base for the purpose of encouraging an immediate purchase.

The Basics

Providing the customer base with complimenting information from other affiliates is also beneficial for the customer.

Through the email marketing strategies, information taking the form of email newsletters can be both informative and relationship building as the customer will be kept well informed while at the same time addressing the customers' needs.

Transactional emails are also helpful in providing the means for the customer to respond accordingly to the merchant, such as dropped basket messages, purchases, order confirmations and many more.

The direct emails are mainly used for the purpose of informing customers of current promotions, announcements, momentary special services available among others.

Most individuals using this tool have found it to be very helpful in tracking the returns on investments and its often only second best to search marketing.

Being able to reach a wider audience base is also another positive attribute of this emailing tool. Countering these, are also disadvantages which contribute to the ineffectiveness of the whole process. This includes the ability of the customers being able to block mails and also the possibility of contravening spam laws.

Chapter 2:
Getting Subscribers

Synopsis

Having a substantial email list is very important to the success of any internet business venture. This is more so because most of the customer base begins through this portal. There all measures should be taken to ensure the subscribers list is long and beneficial to both parties.

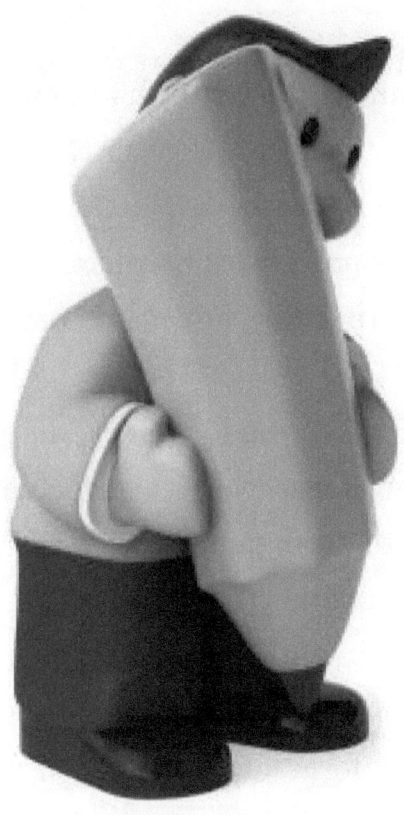

Sign Ups

There are a few points that should be considered in the quest to garner as many subscribers as possible. Some of which are as follows:

Designing the forms, responses and other interactive tools to be as visible as possible and easily accessible is very important. Providing incentive for potential signups will encourage the viewer to be more inclined to do so. Also providing interesting links that the viewer may find useful will eventually lead to the viewer signing up to gain access.

Being constantly aware of what is being offered and how it's being offered will also allow the host to stay abreast and relevant which in turn will attract more subscribers. Material posted should be kept updated periodically as potential subscribers will be drawn to the site more often if this feature is diligently monitored.

In order to be able to constantly attract the attention needed to ensure a good percentage of subscribers there are several complimenting tools that can be used such as through blogs, forum postings, other lists, networking and many more.

The blogs should provide good and interesting information which should include some form of participation from the viewer to encourage a signup.

Forum posting are also another platform to explore as those who visit such sites already have a pre existing interest in the subject matter.

Therefore including links that direct them back to one's site will be advantages in converting them into subscribers. Forwarded emails are also an excellent source of garnering potential subscribers as it gives a glimpse into the individual's site.

Chapter 3:
Reducing Unsubscribes

Synopsis

Most people become tagged as unsubscribers because of the initial bombardment of emails that cause them to be unresponsive. This unresponsiveness can be due to a variety of reasons but the most common one would be simply being fed up with unwanted solicitation or thinly veiled sales pitches. Therefore in order to limit the situation one should be weary of causing potential respondents from being unresponsive.

Get Them To Stay

Here are some ways to adopt to limit the unsubscribers:

- Keep all emails on the topic promised. If there is a need to insert other material keeping it brief would be prudent. The visitor is probably only visiting the site for specific reasons and does not want to be deluged with other non related issues.

- Using the personalized address system in the auto responder will create the illusion of making the individual feel special and respected. The use of names is a good tool to exploit and cannot be overdone or over emphasized.

- Limiting the amount of emails sent in a week to about two or three would be ideal. Too many emails with the same content would not only become a nuisance to the receiver but the information would be redundant too. Too many emails will overwhelm the receiver and thus eventually cause them to be unresponsive. Allowing the customers to choose the frequency of emails sent to them will also encourage better relationships. The customer perceives the sender to be professional and committed.

- Avoid hard selling at the onset of the email exchange. Directing the subscriber to the website where an informative and in-depth presentation can be viewed will allow the viewer to feel more comfortable and convinced to sign on. The website material should be designed to sufficiently "sell" the featured items. However it should be noted that keeping a longer period between emails sent is also not encouraged as the idea is to keep the website relevant to the subscriber.

Chapter 4:
Using Transactional Emails

Synopsis

Emails are ideally supposed to keep the relationship between sender and receiver fresh and relevant al all times. Therefore care should be taken not to embellish this rather delicate relationship.

The Balance

In order to use transactional emails to its optimum benefit, some of the following points should be considered:

Personalized greeting is always a sure winner. Generally people are happy to be considered special thus addressing the emails accordingly, successfully gives this impression.

This is especially so when the element of exchange of money and goods are involved.

Including as much detail as possible without being too boring is also another feature that should be noted in the transactional email style. Callously thanking the sender for a positive response will not be sufficient.

Depicting the details will ensure both parties are in agreement with what is to transpire and it also helps to avoid future misunderstandings and problems.

Always ensure the customer support contact details are clearly displayed such as toll free phone numbers, mailing addresses, links to online contacts and any other relevant information the customer may need.

There is nothing more frustrating for the customer when such information is not forth coming.

The transactional emails should also include a link to the home page easily, as there maybe a variety of reasons the customer may need to make some reference to the original material available only on the home page.

Some find it useful to also include other feature like email newsletters and special promotions and offers. Also popularly included are RSS feeds for updated information and products. Loyalty programs, customer forums, blogs, social-network sites are also recommended to be included for added advantage.

Sometimes there is a need to include guidelines on the item's use and makeup which is helpful to the receiving party. This will help to cut down the time spent trying to decipher the product's functions.

Chapter 5:
Using Triggers In The Email

Synopsis

Perhaps understanding what this tool is first before deciding to use it should be explored for obvious benefits. Simply explained, triggers are pieces of SQL which causes activation when certain events or actions occur. When new data is inserted into a program the user is able stay abreast with these new developments through the triggers as and when they are activated.

Triggers

These triggers are very useful when compared to the task of having to individually alert subscribers to new materials available. An ideal trigger template should include the following items like creating the trigger (new menu) SQL, using specific value for template parameters, commands (Ctrl-Shift-M) which fill the parameter and other more technical needs.

Triggers in emails allow the time frame for the marketing pitch to be suited to the customer's needs without having to assert too much effort.

This trigger based platform is both effective and precise in assisting the marketing programs to seize the moments and make an impact.

This provides the hosting party to be able to entice the customer at just the right time with just the right amount of knowledge so as not to be perceived as pushy and thus off putting.

Not requiring any constant monitoring is also another reason for the popularity of the trigger tool. These triggers are ideals as complimenting partners to broader programs like newsletters, special offers and acquisition programs.

This is made more attractive because it is primarily activated through customer behavioral patterns. Because the customer initiating action is the focal point of the triggers the responses are also more likely to be favorable. It has been noted that the results have been encouraging and customer satisfaction rates have improved.

There has been a documented improvement in response rates when compared to the more conventional emailing campaigns. This of course is good news to those concerned about bombarding their emailing listed customers into submission.

Chapter 6:
Testing Different Variations Of Your Email

Synopsis

Already noted is the fact that email campaigns are for most the focal point of the business harnessing tools. Therefore it is interesting and exciting to note that this particular tool can be changed constantly until desired results are met. Testing the many variations possible for the email format design can be quite a challenge but none the less a rewarding one.

Check It Out

Below are just some of the areas where the variable theory can be applied:

Starting from the basics would be the exercise of finding the best suited and result proven sender information. Finding the suitable name, company name, keyword or any other addressing term that denotes branding building and recognition is important.

When this is successfully identified it should be kept and used consistently and without further change unless deemed necessary and beneficial.

The subject line also has to be measured for its opening rate until the most suitable combination is found.

The same concept should be applied to the measurement of the click rate and conversion rate for the content element. These should include the different variances for personalization, wording, call to action, layout, numbers, placements, images, lengths and many other connective content matters.

Gauging the opening rates based on the times of a day is also another variant that can and should be tried out.

In identifying the "peak" opening times the host will be better positioned for business.

Varying the landing pages content to suit the needs of the possible masses is also recommended. Designing the landing pages to be attractive enough to encourage further interest is vital to getting click converted to committed customers.

Ultimately the idea should be to keep the customer engaged within the initial click on the landing page without too many complicated follow up steps.

Chapter 7:
Use Analytics To Separate Buyers From Non Buyers

Synopsis

The success of online businesses depends largely on the exposure rate and impact the website makes on the visitor. This is very important to the first impression being formed as the merchant does not have the luxury of personal contact to gauge the customer's wants and needs of the time. Therefore tools like information derived from analysis would have a rather profound impact on the online business success rate.

Gauge It

Some of the items that should be considered when creating a conducive platform to encourage transactions would be to know some basic information on the demographics intended.

This information should cover geographical locations, family makeup, buying power and it should help to identify the target buyer.

Serious buyers would essentially be looking into important elements like measurable quantitative terms, substantial availability of items, accessible distribution methods, sensitive and well planned affordable marketing exposure that generates the right kind of interest.

Well designed internet tools will help to detect the interest rates as their frequency and active purchases are logged. Buyer will also generally stay loyal if and when the products sought are able to maintain the promised quality and quantity without doubt.

Non buyers however will only be interested in browsing for the cheapest deals and may not necessarily make a purchase in the end.

Serious buyers also tend to be more active in surfing for the most compatible and innovative items available. These individual will stay focus and true to the intention of making a purchase thus taking the trouble to source the relevant information where and when needed.

There are several tools already available to be utilized when there is a need to track such behavioral patterns to ensure the right target audience is being reached. All this is based mostly on addressing the niche marketing sector.

Chapter 8:
Use Loyalty Programs

Synopsis

Having a good and strong customer base is very important to the success of any business venture. Therefore it is important to ensure the customer base stays as loyal as possible as this in turn helps to create some form of stability for the merchant.

Keep Them Coming Back

Perhaps the among the most effective ways of creating and maintaining the customer loyalty ratios lies in the ability to provide as many incentives as possible through the setting up of various loyalty programs.

These loyalty programs should ideally be able to increase the customer's interest in staying with the product over a long period of time, thus repeat purchases become a norm.

The loyalty programs should ideally give the customer the satisfaction of knowing the merchant is interested in creating an environment where the customer is encouraged to be a major part of the business.

This inclusion makes the customer feel important and considered and it also inspires the customer to stay loyal as the rewards for past purchases are tagged to the next purchase.

The loyalty programs are usually designed according to information that may include information on buying patterns and preferences of the customers.

Buy ahead discounts, purchase level rewards, rebates based on spending levels, upgrades or special added benefits are all different incentives that can be included in the loyalty program to make it as enticing as possible.

The buy ahead discounts are designed to ensure the customer is locked in from the very beginning when a purchase is made. This may be done in the form of a loyalty card that entitles the purchaser to enjoy immediate discounts or free gifts with future purchases.

The other popular loyalty program item is the rebates on spending levels where the purchaser is given bigger discounts when the purchase amount passes the relevant levels.

Chapter 9:
Determine The Correct Frequency To Send Emails

Synopsis

The question of frequency is always as issue and here are some tips to assist in making a more informed decision.

Important Decision

Testing is one good way to start. Besides observing market trends and available information on the subject, there is a need to conduct a series of test of the various frequency rates before a suitable one is found.

Feedback is an important and valuable assisting tool to provide the information that can help make decisions which affect the business.

Soliciting feedback is usually not easy as most people would rather not take the time to respond to this but if persistent there will eventually be a response that can provide valuable information like if the material featured is too boring and lack helpful information or if the frequency of receiving the mail is perceived to be annoying or if the content is totally irrelevant or of no interest to the recipient.

If market conditions or seasonal shopping is the prime factor in the particular business being touted then some thought should be given to whether the recipient's needs are being properly addressed in the material sent.

There is a fine line between sending too much too quickly and sending too little and too infrequently for this particular niche. How experience can and usually does play a pivotal role in deciding contents and frequency.

Giving the receiving party a chance to participate in the decision on the frequency of the emails received is also another option worth exploring.

Most recipients will be happy to oblige with such information and this will in turn create the interest and eagerness for both parties in sending and receiving the intended material.

Wrapping Up

Getting the business on a recognizable platform is important but doing it in a way that brings about the opposite results is detrimental to the success of the business. Emails are an important yet tricky tool and should be carefully considered before any decision is made. The question of frequency is always as issue and here we have provided some tips to assist in making a more informed decision.

www.ingramcontent.com/pod-product-compliance
Lightning Source LLC
Chambersburg PA
CBHW030553220526
45463CB00007B/3077